# Piano Technique

## Book 1

*Authors*

**Barbara Kreader, Fred Kern, Phillip Keveren, Mona Rejino**

*Editor*
Carol Klose

*Illustrator*
Fred Bell

ISBN 978-0-634-00426-1

**HAL•LEONARD**®

Copyright © 2000 by HAL LEONARD CORPORATION
International Copyright Secured   All Rights Reserved

Visit Hal Leonard Online at
**www.halleonard.com**

World headquarters, contact:
**Hal Leonard**
7777 West Bluemound Road
Milwaukee, WI 53213
Email: info@halleonard.com

In Europe, contact:
**Hal Leonard Europe Limited**
Dettingen Way
Bury St Edmunds, Suffolk, IP33 3YB
Email: info@halleonardeurope.com

In Australia, contact:
**Hal Leonard Australia Pty. Ltd.**
4 Lentara Court
Cheltenham, Victoria, 3192 Australia
Email: info@halleonard.com.au

## CONTENTS

| | | Technique Book | Lesson Book |
|---|---|---|---|
| ✔ | | | |

*\* Students can check activities as they complete them.*

Dear Teacher,

**Piano Technique Book 1** presents a *Warm-Up* and an *Etude* for each new technical skill students will encounter in **Piano Lessons Book 1**.

We suggest that you demonstrate each *Warm-Up*. Teaching by demonstration allows students to focus on the purely physical aspects of learning a new skill, such as hand and body position, or arm and finger movement. This helps them understand the connection between the movement they make and the sound they create.

Once students have learned the physical skill presented in each *Warm-Up*, they can use it to play the corresponding *Etude* with expression.

The *Musical Fitness Plan* on each warm-up page teaches new technical concepts and provides a check list for technical readiness:

- **Body and Hand Position**
- **Beautiful Tone**
- **Attention to Silence**
- **Dynamics**
- **Detached Tones**
- **Connected Tones**

By the end of **Piano Technique Book 1**, students will be able to produce a full-sounding tone with every finger and will be ready to play *staccato, legato,* and hands together using different fingers in each hand. Having mastered these skills, students will have the confidence to move on to the technical challenges presented in **Piano Lessons Book 2**.

Best wishes,

*Barbara Kreader    Fred Kern*

*Phillip Keveren    Mona Rejino*

Dear Students,

You need an exercise plan to stay physically fit.

Like participating in sports, playing the piano is a physical activity that uses your whole body. **Piano Technique Book 1** will outline the *Musical Fitness Plan* you need to develop new musical skills.

Your *Musical Fitness Plan* includes:

- **Warm-Ups** – drills to develop new musical skills
- **Etudes** – music to practice using the new skills you learned in the *Warm-Ups*

It feels good to play the piano! Your teacher will show you how to play each *Warm-Up*. Follow the *Musical Fitness Plan*, paying careful attention to the way you use your body, arms, and fingers to create music. When you play, notice how the movement you make affects the sound you create. Once you have learned each *Warm-Up*, read and practice the matching *Etude*.

Before beginning any work at the piano, it is important to notice how you are **SITTING AT THE PIANO**.

Ask yourself:

- Am I sitting tall but staying relaxed?
- Are my wrists and elbows level with the keys of the piano?

You are now ready to begin.

Have fun!

*Barbara Kreader    Fred Kern*

*Phillip Keveren    Mona Rejino*

# Musical Fitness Plan

**Use this checklist to review fitness skills and to focus on learning new ones.**

 *NEW!*

## Hand Position
Let your arms and hands hang naturally at your sides. Notice the curve of your fingers. Keep this position as you place your fingers on the black keys.

 *NEW!*

## Beautiful Tone
Use equal weight from each arm as you play.

 *NEW!*

## Attention to Silence
In *Long Shadows* and *Locomotion*, release your arm weight during each rest, keeping your fingers on the keys.

*To the Teacher: Demonstrate these black key warm-ups. Encourage your student to play them in different octaves up and down the piano keyboard.*

# Warm-Ups

### Grandfather's Clock *pg. 4*
(Using whole arm)

*Notice in the picture how the grandfather clock uses his arms to sway from side to side.*

As you play this warm-up, pretend you are the clock by using your whole arm weight as you play, *"left, right, left, right."*

Experiment by playing the warm-up "way down low" then "way up high" on the keyboard.

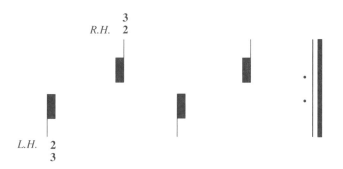

### Long Shadows *pg. 5*
(Using whole arm and individual fingers)

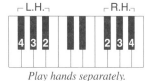

*Play hands separately.*

*The boy in the picture is carefully balancing on one foot.*

Play the clusters using your whole arm and then balance on one finger. Feel how your arm weight shifts easily from three fingers to one finger.

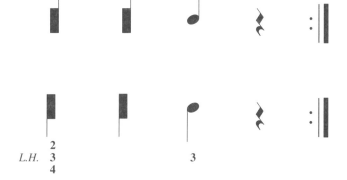

### Locomotion *pg. 6*
(Repeating and stepping)

When playing repeated-note patterns, let your wrist bounce lightly as you play each key.

Like train cars on a track, the music in *Locomotion* travels from one note to the next. Keep your fingers on the keys during each rest so that the train will stay on its track!

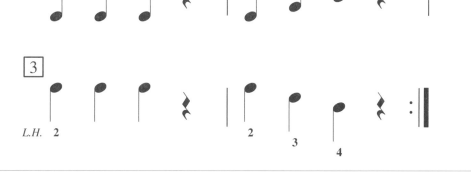

3

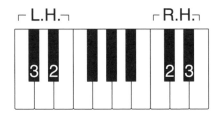

# Grandfather's Clock

Keep "ticking" to the end.

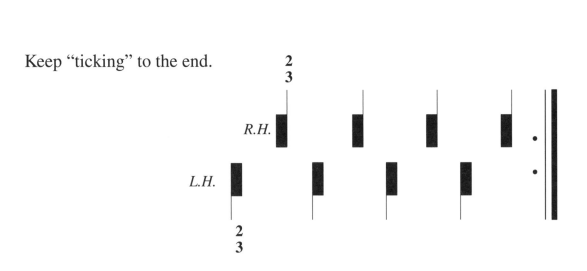

With accompaniment, student starts here:

Henry Clay Work

Tick Tock (♩=100)

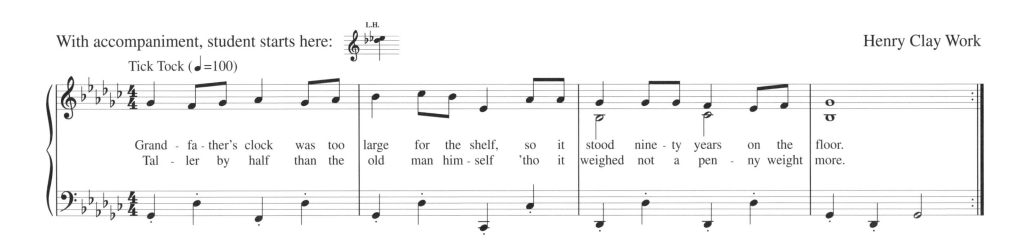

Grand – fa - ther's clock was too large for the shelf, so it stood nine - ty years on the floor.
Tal - ler by half than the old man him - self 'tho it weighed not a pen – ny weight more.

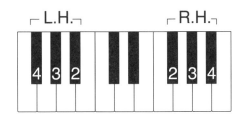

# Long Shadows

Slowly

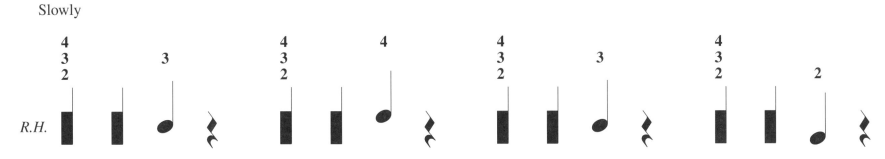

*R.H.*

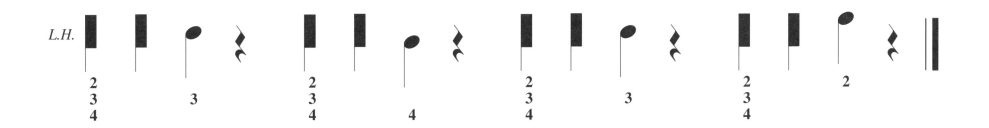

*L.H.*

With accompaniment, student starts here:

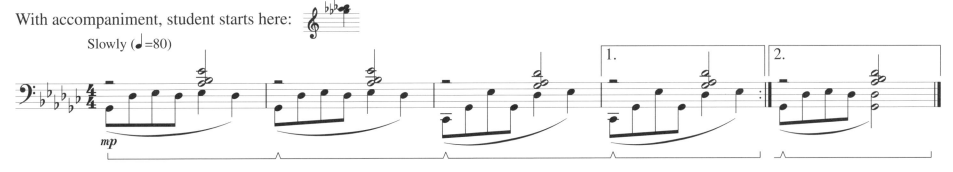

Slowly (♩=80)

*mp*

*Use with Lesson Book 1, pgs. 14-15*

5

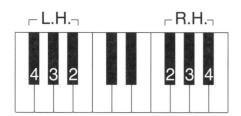

# Locomotion

Steady

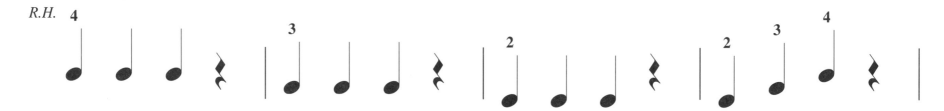

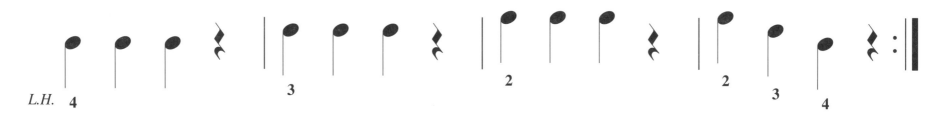

With accompaniment, student starts here:

Steady (♩=120)

*Use with Lesson Book 1, pgs. 16-20*

# Musical Fitness Plan

 **NEW!**

## Hand Position

In *The Attic Stairs*, support the first joint of your third finger with your thumb.

When playing with your thumb, such as in *Look At Me* and *Monster Under My Bed*,  let it rest naturally on the outside tip.

 **NEW!**

## Beautiful Tone

Use weight from your whole arm as you play each key. Let your arm follow your fingers.

☐ **Attention to Silence**

 **NEW!**

## Playing *Forte*

Press the key to the bottom of the key bed with full arm weight.

 **NEW!**

## Playing *Piano*

Press the key to the bottom of the key bed with less arm weight.

*To the Teacher:* Demonstrate these white key warm-ups. Encourage your student to play the same exercise with the opposite hand (using opposite fingering).

# Warm-Ups

### The Attic Stairs *pg. 8*
(Whole arm with supported third finger)

*Imagine you are climbing up attic stairs.*

With your whole arm weight behind the third finger, move slowly and steadily up the piano keys. Begin on the **A** below Middle **C**.
1. Play **R.H.** alone, finger 3, in whole notes.
2. Play **L.H.** alone, finger 3, in whole notes.

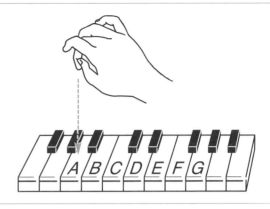

### Look At Me! *pg. 9*
(Play and release)

*Notice how the young girl leans into her step as she marches with confidence.*

Play with your right hand. Play a *forte* sound by leaning into each key with full arm weight.

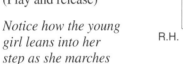

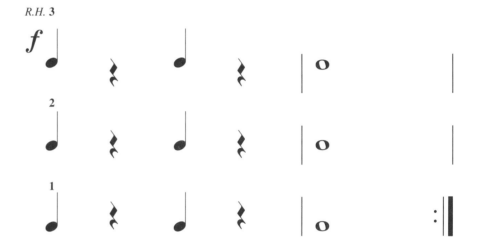

### Monster Under My Bed *pg. 10*
(Playing *piano* and *forte*)

*The monster groans with his soft voice, then suddenly roars with his loud voice.*

Copy the monster by leaning into each key with less arm weight for his soft voice (first line, *p*) and leaning into each key with full arm weight for his loud voice (second line, *f*).

Play with your left hand.

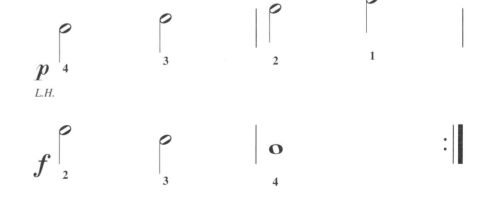

# The Attic Stairs

Sing the musical alphabet forward and backward as you play "The Attic Stairs." Keep your thumb behind the first joint of your third finger.

Climb the stairs **two** times. Use finger 3.
  1. R.H. alone.
  2. L.H. alone.

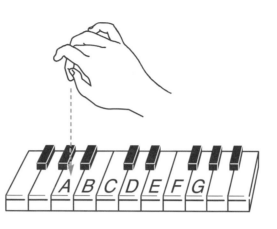

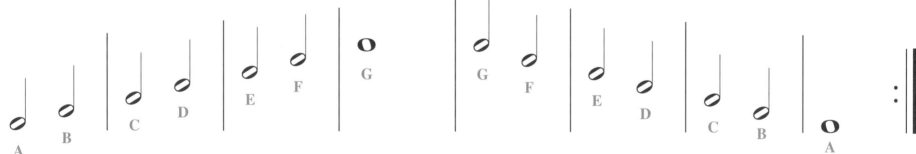

With accompaniment, student starts here:

Slowly (♩=100)

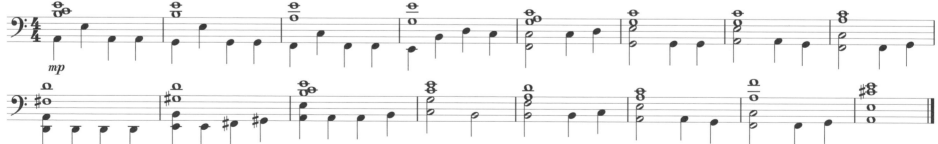

*mp*

*Use with Lesson Book 1, pg. 21*

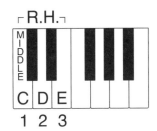

# Look At Me!

March

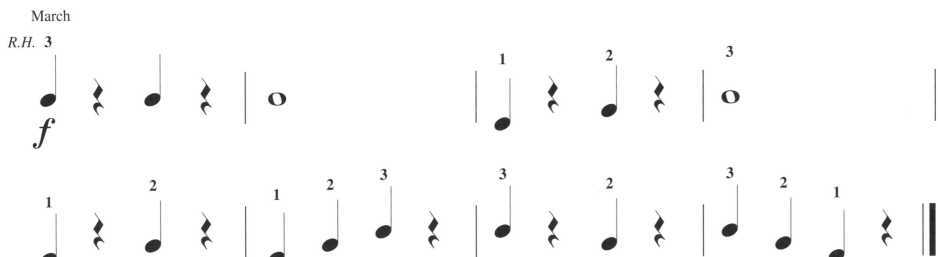

With accompaniment, student starts here:

March (♩=110)

*Use with Lesson Book 1, pgs. 24-25*

9

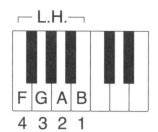

# Monster Under My Bed

Scary

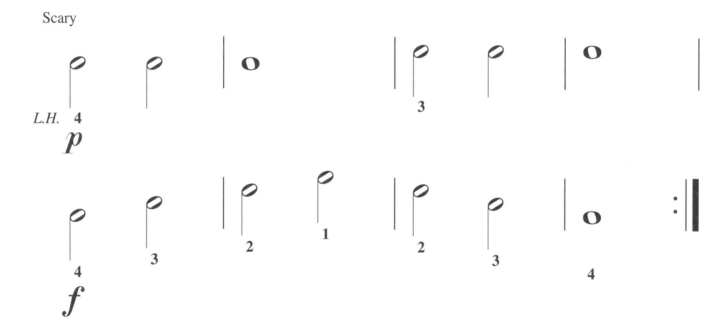

L.H.  4

*p*

4  3  2  1  2  3  4

*f*

With accompaniment, student starts here:

Scary (♩=86)

*pp  poco a poco cresc.*

*mf*

*Use with Lesson Book 1, pgs. 28-29*

10

# Musical Fitness Plan

**Use this checklist to review fitness skills and to focus on learning new ones.**

 **NEW!**

## Hand Position
Raise your hand and wave to your teacher with your fingers. Notice how your fingers move from the knuckles *(bridge)*. As you press each key, play from the *bridge* of the hand with each finger.

☐ **Attention to Silence**

☐ **Playing *Forte***

☐ **Playing *Piano***

 **NEW!**

## Connected Tones
Pass the sound smoothly from finger to finger and hand to hand.

 **NEW!**

## Detached Tones
Release the key as soon as you play it, letting your wrist bounce lightly. Notice how your finger naturally rebounds and comes to rest on the key.

*To the Teacher: Demonstrate these warm-ups. Encourage your student to play them starting on different white keys. This is an excellent opportunity for the student to discover musical shapes and sequences.*

# Warm-Ups

**Breathe Easy** *pg. 12*
(Connecting tones)

*Inhale slowly, then exhale in one deep breath. Notice how your breath flows smoothly in and out without a pause.*

Create the feeling of a long, connected breath within the music. As you play the warm-up, inhale on the first four counts and exhale on the next four counts.

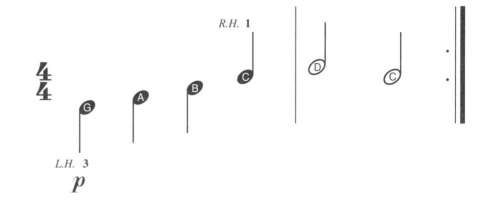

**Playing Catch** *pg. 13*
(Moving the sound from hand to hand)

*A juggler tosses a ball from hand to hand with an equal motion.*

*Repeat, using:*
*R.H. 3 - L.H. 3*
*R.H. 4- L.H. 4*
*Play R.H. 8va higher*

Imitate that same motion on the piano as you move the sound from hand to hand.

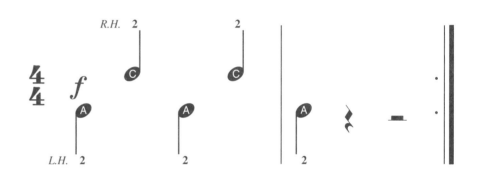

**Popcorn** *pg. 14*
(Using whole arm, skipping and separating tones)

*Imitate the sound of corn popping.*

Play each note so that it has a short sound. Release each key as soon as you play it. Let your finger rebound and come to rest on the same key. Listen carefully for the space between each tone.

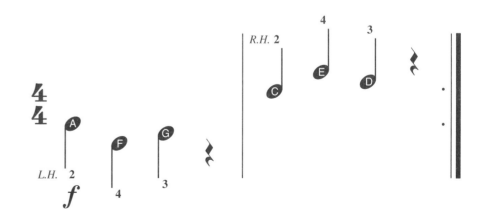

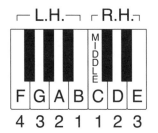

# Breathe Easy

Smoothly

*R.H.* **3**

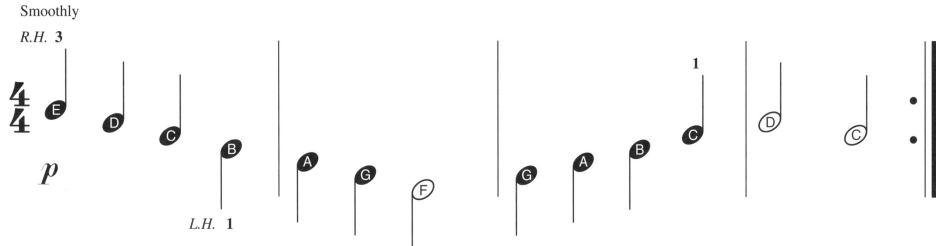

*L.H.* **1**

With accompaniment, student starts here:

Smoothly (♩=86)

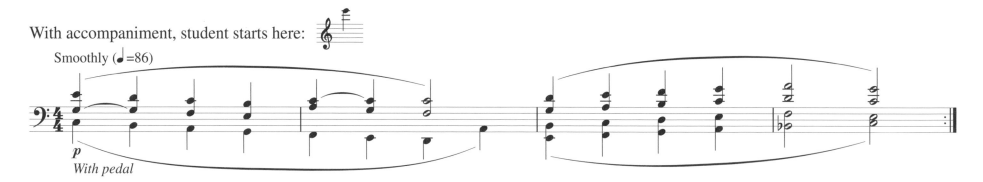

*p*

*With pedal*

*Use with Lesson Book 1, pg. 30*

12

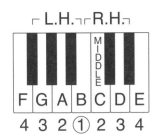

# Playing Catch

Back and forth

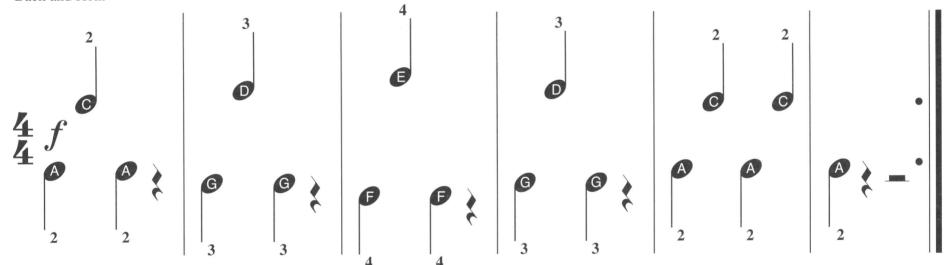

With accompaniment, student starts here:

Back and forth (♩=110)

*Use with Lesson Book 1, pgs. 31-32*

13

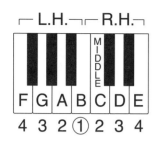

# Popcorn

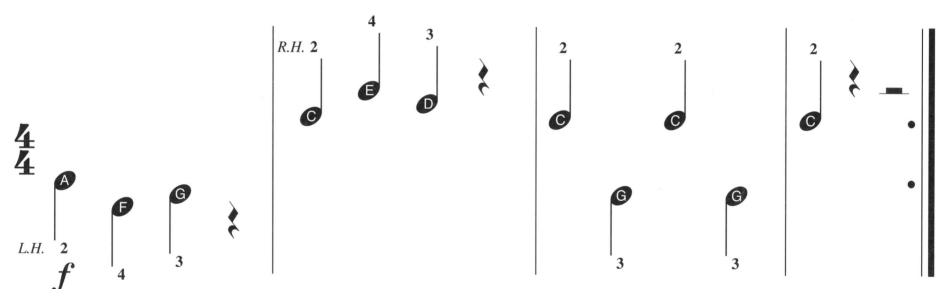

With accompaniment, student starts here:

Bouncy (♩=110)

*Use with Lesson Book 1, pgs. 33-34*

14

# Musical Fitness Plan

**Use this checklist to review fitness skills and to focus on learning new ones.**

☐ **Hand Position**

☐ **Beautiful Tone**

☐ **Attention to Silence**

☐ **Playing** *Forte*

☐ **Playing** *Piano*

☐ **Connected Tones**

☐ **Detached Tones**

*To the Teacher: Demonstrate these warm-ups. Encourage your student to play them in different octaves up and down the keyboard.*

## Warm-Ups

**Hot Sand Hop** *pg. 16*
(Separating tones)

**Molding Clay** *pg. 17*
(Connecting tones)

**Sneaky Footsteps** *pg. 18*
(Separating tones)

**Fingerpainting** *pg. 19*
(Connecting tones)

**On The Balance Beam** *pg. 20*
(Connecting melodies)

*While stepping gracefully on a balance beam, a gymnast smoothly transfers body weight from one leg to the other.*

Balance the *piano* sound as you pass the melody between your two hands.

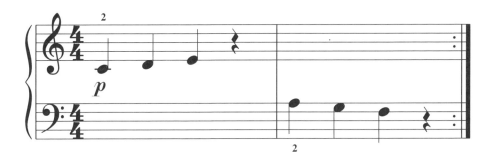

**Star To Star** *pg. 21*
(Connecting steps from hand to hand)

*A skater glides smoothly across the ice by shifting weight from one foot to the other.*

When you play, make the sound shift from one note to the next so smoothly that no one can tell where one hand begins and the other ends.

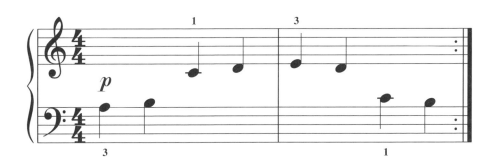

# Hot Sand Hop

Too hot!

$f$ ⁴

**Accompaniment** (Student plays one octave higher than written.)

Too hot! (♩=120)

*mf*

*Use with Lesson Book 1, pg. 38*

# Molding Clay

Smoothly

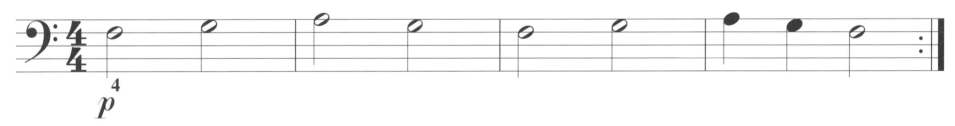

*p*

**Accompaniment** (Student plays one octave higher than written.)

Smoothly (♩=96)

*pp*

*Use with Lesson Book 1, pg. 38*

# Sneaky Footsteps

On tiptoe

**Accompaniment** (Student plays one octave higher than written.)

On tiptoe ($\quarternote$=120)

*Use with Lesson Book 1, pg. 40*

18

# Fingerpainting

Smoothly

**Accompaniment** (Student plays one octave higher than written.)

Smoothly (♩=96)

*Use with Lesson Book 1, pg. 41*

# On The Balance Beam

Gracefully

Move right | grace - ful - ly. | Move left | care - ful - ly.

Right foot first, | then the left. | Care - ful not to | fall.

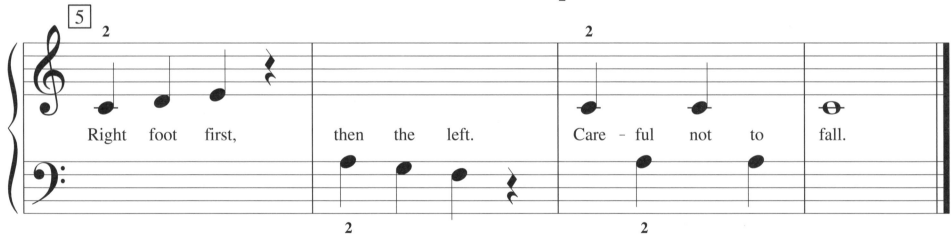

**Accompaniment** (Student plays one octave higher than written.)

Gracefully (♩=80)

*Use with Lesson Book 1, pg. 43*

# Star To Star

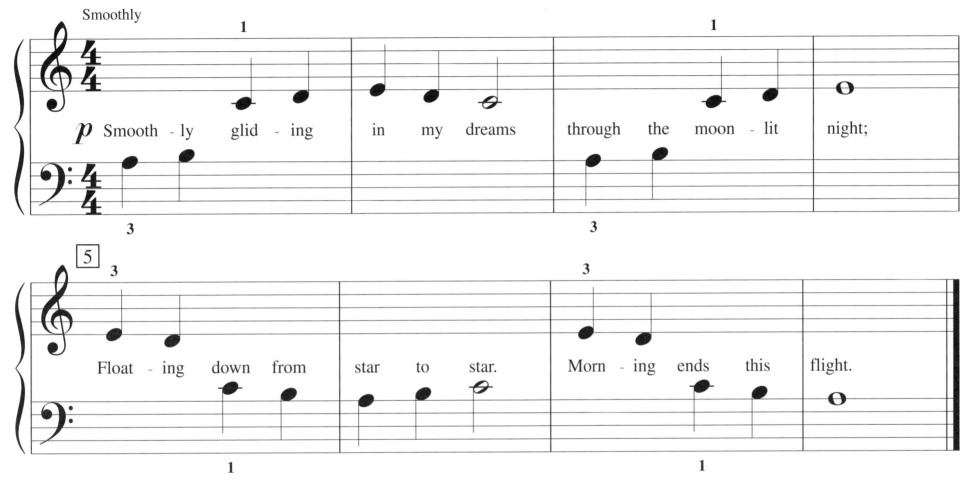

Smoothly

*p* Smooth - ly glid - ing | in my dreams | through the moon - lit | night;

Float - ing down from | star to star. | Morn - ing ends this | flight.

**Accompaniment** (Student plays one octave higher than written.)

Smoothly (♩=76)

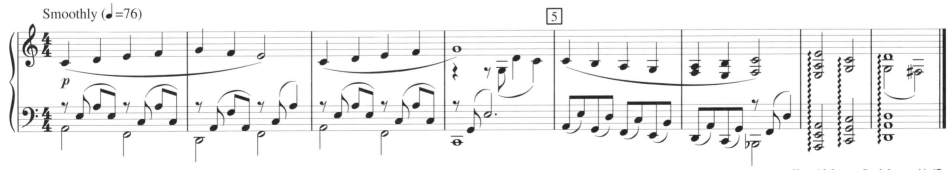

*Use with Lesson Book 1, pgs. 44-47*

# Musical Fitness Plan

Use this checklist to review fitness skills and to focus on learning new ones.

☐ **Hand Position**

☐ **Beautiful Tone**

☐ **Attention to Silence**

 *NEW!*

**Playing** *Mezzo Forte*
Press the key to the bottom of the key bed with medium arm weight. Listen to the sound you create.

☐ **Playing** *Forte*

☐ **Playing** *Piano*

☐ **Connected Tones**

☐ **Detached Tones**

*To the Teacher: Demonstrate these warm-ups. Encourage your student to experiment by playing in other positions (by changing octaves, creating musical sequences, etc.).*

## Warm-Ups

**Who Could It Be?** *pg. 23*
(Syncopation)

On the closed piano lid, tap the rhythm of the title:

**Who  Could  It    Be?**

Let your wrist bounce lightly on the first note then lean firmly into the next note.

In the warm-up, play *forte* with your left hand, then *piano* with your right hand.

---

**Ping Pong, Anyone?** *pgs. 24-25*
(Alternating repeated notes)

When you play repeated-note patterns, let your wrist bounce lightly like a ping-pong ball. Release each key as soon as you play it. Let your finger rebound and come to rest on the same key.

## Ping          Pong

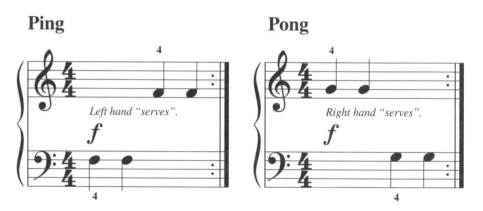

Using the same notes, play "Ping" and "Pong" with:
L.H. 3 - R.H. 3     L.H. 2 - R.H. 2     L.H. 1 - R.H. 1.

---

**On My Way** *pg. 26*
(Connecting skips from hand to hand)

Keep the sound connected as you pass the melody from finger to finger, and from hand to hand.

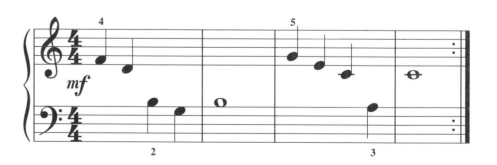

# Who Could It Be?

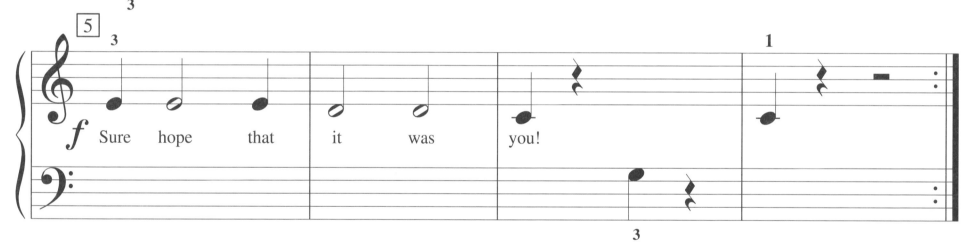

**Accompaniment** (Student plays two octaves higher than written.)

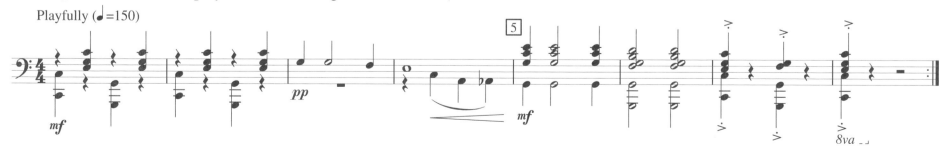

*Use with Lesson Book 1, pgs. 48-49*

# Ping Pong, Anyone?

## Ping

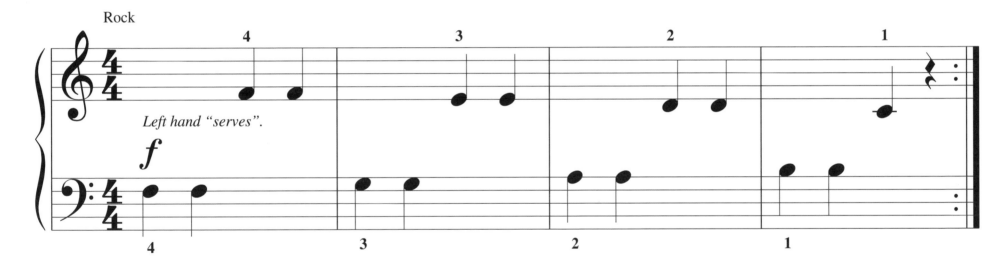

Rock

Left hand "serves".

$f$

**Accompaniment** (Student plays one octave higher than written.)

Rock ($\quad$=110)

*mf*

*Use with Lesson Book 1, pg. 51*

# Pong

'n' roll

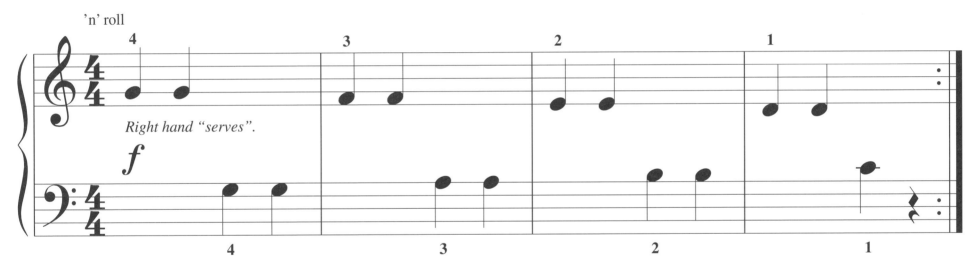

*Right hand "serves".*

**Accompaniment** (Student plays one octave higher than written.)

'n' roll (♩=110)

*Use with Lesson Book 1, pg. 51*

25

# On My Way

Happily

*mf* Step by step I'm | off to school, | whist - ling on my | way.

Skip - ping home now; | school is out! | No more work, I'm | free to play.

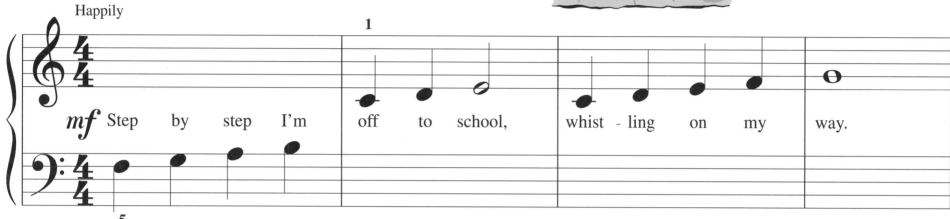

**Accompaniment** (Student plays one octave higher than written.)

Happily (♩=105)

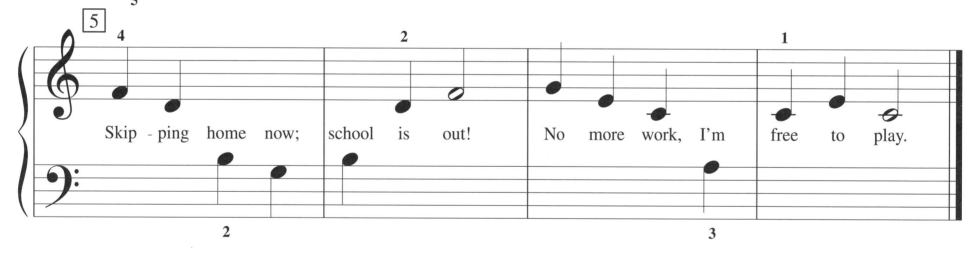

*Use with Lesson Book 1, pg. 51*

26

# Musical Fitness Plan

Use this checklist to review fitness skills and to focus on learning new ones.

- ☐ **Hand Position**
- ☐ **Beautiful Tone**
- ☐ **Attention to Silence**
- ☐ **Playing** *Mezzo Forte*
- ☐ **Playing** *Piano*

*NEW!*

**Playing** *Mezzo Piano*
Press the key to the bottom of the key bed with slightly less arm weight. Listen to the sound you create.

- ☐ **Connected Tones**
- ☐ **Detached Tones**

## Warm-Ups

**Dreaming And Drifting** *pg. 28*
(Alternating skips)

*Imagine how it feels to sway gently in a hammock.*

As you play this warm-up, let your arm follow the movement of your fingers from side to side.

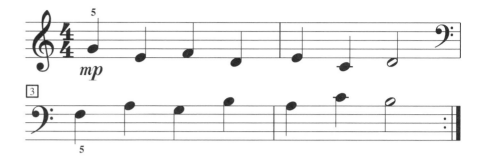

**Happy Heart** *pg. 29*
(Separating skips)

Let your wrist bounce lightly on each key. Listen carefully for the space between each note.

**Waterslide** *pgs. 30-31*
(Connecting patterns of steps and skips)

*Imagine gliding around curves on a slippery waterslide.*

Shape your own waterslide by passing the sound smoothly from finger to finger. Notice the different dynamic levels.

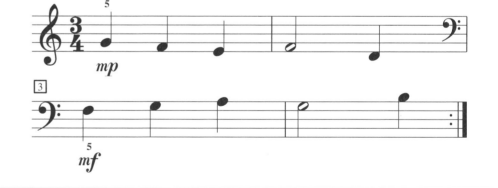

**Ready To Go** *pg. 32*
(Playing skips in syncopation)

Let your arm follow the movement of your fingers. Create a *forte* sound by using your full arm weight.

Repeat, using L.H. 4 - 2 on the same notes.

# Dreaming And Drifting

Gently rocking

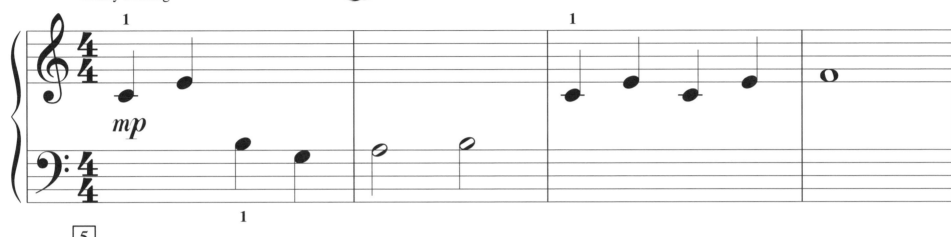

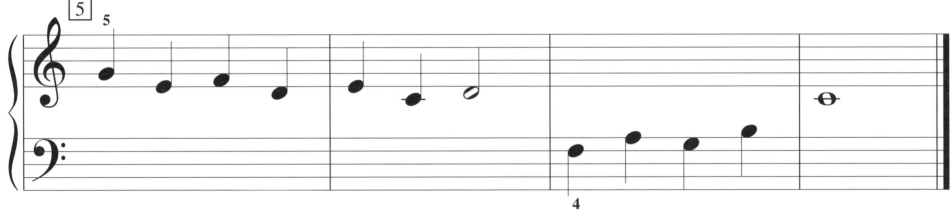

**Accompaniment** (Student plays two octaves higher than written.)

Gently rocking (♩=80)

With pedal

*Use with Lesson Book 1, pgs. 52-54*

# Happy Heart

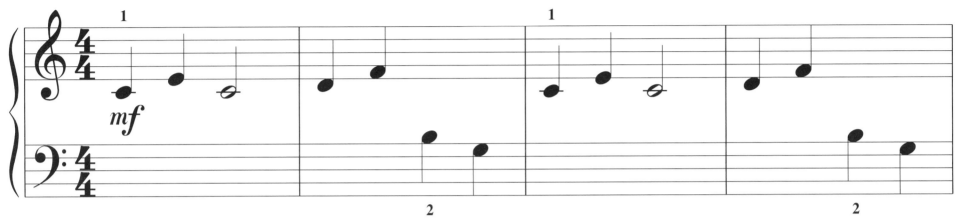

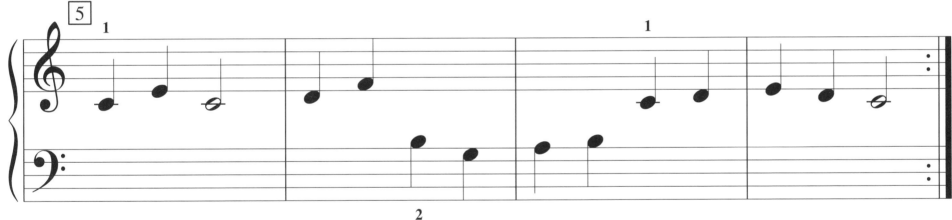

**Accompaniment** (Student plays one octave higher than written.)

*Use with Lesson Book 1, pgs. 56-57*

# Waterslide

Slippery

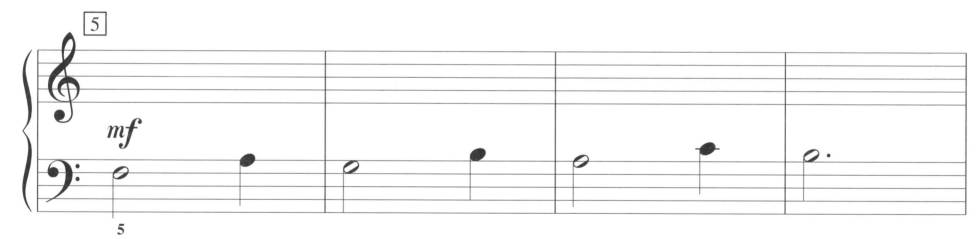

**Accompaniment**

Slippery (♩=115)

*Use with Lesson Book 1, pgs. 59-61*

30

# Ready To Go

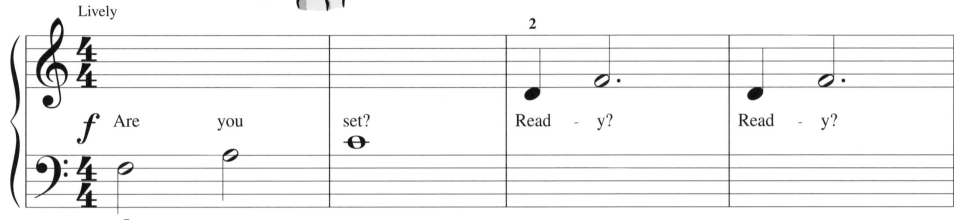

Lively

$f$ Are you set? Read - y? Read - y?

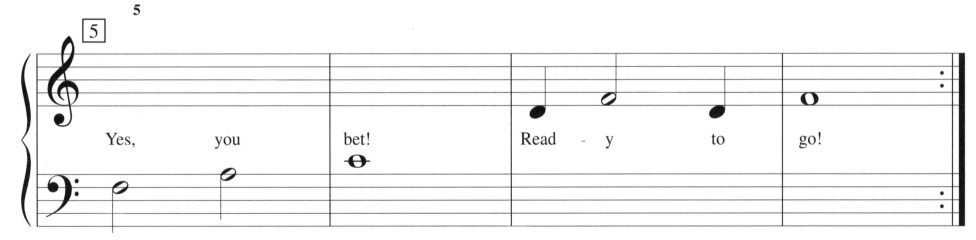

Yes, you bet! Read - y to go!

**Accompaniment** (Student plays one octave higher than written.)

Lively ($\half$=100)

*Use with Lesson Book 1, pgs. 62-63*

32